MY N

C000067806

MOBY

Written by Dawn McMillan
Illustrated by Connah Brecon

Little Mead Academy Trust
Company no. 08245853; limited by guarantee and registered in England & Wales
Registered office: Gosforth Road, Southmead, Bristol, BS10 6DS

Published by Pearson Education Limited, 80 Strand, London, WC2R 0RL.

www.pearsonschools.co.uk

First published in 2010 by Pearson Australia.
This edition of *My Name Is Moby* is published by Pearson Education Limited
by arrangement with Pearson Australia. All rights reserved.

Text © Pearson Australia 2010
Text by Dawn McMillan

Original illustrations © Pearson Australia 2010
Illustrated by Connah Brecon

22 21 20 19 18
10 9 8 7 6 5 4 3 2 1

British Library Cataloguing in Publication Data
A catalogue record for this book is available from the British Library

ISBN 978 0 435 19423 9

Printed in China by Golden Cup

Acknowledgements
We would like to thank the following schools for their invaluable help in the
development and trialling of the Bug Club resources: Bishop Road Primary
School, Bristol; Blackhorse Primary School, Bristol; Hollingwood Primary School,
West Yorkshire; Kingswood Parks Primary, Hull; Langdale CE Primary School,
Ambleside; Pickering Infant School, Pickering; The Royal School, Wolverhampton;
St Thomas More's Catholic Primary School, Hampshire; West Park Primary School,
Wolverhampton.

Note from the publisher
Pearson has robust editorial processes, including answer and fact checks, to ensure
the accuracy of the content in this publication, and every effort is made to ensure
this publication is free of errors. We are, however, only human, and occasionally
errors do occur. Pearson is not liable for any misunderstandings that arise as a
result of errors in this publication, but it is our priority to ensure that the content
is accurate. If you spot an error, please do contact us at resourcescorrections@
pearson.com so we can make sure it is corrected.

CONTENTS

Chapter 1

A SECRET

My name is Moby. It's a bit of a funny name, isn't it? I'm not sure I like it very much.

I wish I was called Jack! Jack is a name with some bounce to it. But I'm stuck with the name of Moby.

My home is with a family of humans.
The largest of them, Simon, has some strange
habits. At the breakfast table, he likes to read
the newspaper and doesn't talk to anyone!
Perhaps he's trying to hide from the others.

When I try to peep behind the paper to see
what he is doing, he tells me to sit down.

"Behave yourself, Moby!" Simon says.
"You'll get your breakfast in a minute!"

Silly man! I'm not thinking about breakfast.
I'm more interested in him!

That's the thing with humans. They believe they know what we dogs are thinking, but of course they don't! Simon seems to think I speak *his* language, though. Sometimes he says, "That Moby! There are times when I think he understands English!"

Well, my reader friends, let me tell you a secret. Dogs don't need to understand English or any other language, because … we're mind-readers!

Being a mind-reader can be pretty tough, sometimes. For example, right now, I know that my family is thinking of moving house. I feel sick. I don't want to move. I'm not a new-house sort of dog.

So – I'm sad. The mother, Kara, is the first to notice that I'm not eating.

"Moby's ill," she says to Simon. "He hasn't touched his food today!"

"Mmm," Simon agrees. "He's not interested in walking either. That's a worry."

They give me lots of attention, now that they think I'm ill. Good! I like that! Olivia and Marcus sit by my side and rub my back.

But – oh dear! Now they're planning something that's no fun at all! They're thinking of taking me to the vet!

I really don't want to go to the vet, and there's only one way to stop that happening.

I have to stop worrying, eat everything they give me and beg for more. I have to wag my tail and look as if I want a walk. I must pretend that everything is okay, until I can think of a plan.

There must be something I can do to stop the family moving!

Chapter 2

TIME FOR A PLAN

I know! I need to make sure no one wants to buy our house. I need a plan that won't hurt anyone.

I'm a good dog and I'm proud of it. I don't want to scare anyone, or bite anyone. I just want to put people off buying our house! But how?

I watch from my kennel and wait for ideas.

Lately, Kara's been keeping the house extra clean and tidy. She's made Olivia and Marcus tidy their rooms, too. I'm not allowed to sleep on the mat inside any more.

This morning, Kara pointed to the door and said, "Outside, Moby! We've got people coming to see the house today. I don't want your hair making a mess all over everything!"

A mess over everything, indeed! The people coming today must be very clean and fancy. Hmm ... that gives me an idea!

Now Kara is spraying a pongy, rosy-smelling spray everywhere, to get rid of my doggy smell. Oh, no! Before all this house-selling stuff, Kara seemed to like the way I smelled! I put my head between my paws.

I feel sad, but now I have a new idea. People don't like doggy smells, or doggy hair all over the place! Perhaps I can use this fact to help me.

I go and see Simon. He's been out in the garden all morning, tidying up. Now he's getting that awful lawnmower out of the shed.

That gives me another idea! Suddenly my plan is complete. I leap up with excitement. Nobody will buy the house while I'm on the case, I'm sure of that!

Chapter 3

DOG HAIR
EVERYWHERE

The buyers are driving towards our house.
I can hear them in the distance.

I need to be careful. I must allow just the
right amount of time to carry out my plan.
I don't want to give Simon and Kara the
chance to spoil it.

My heart is beating loudly. My coat feels damp. Maybe I *do* need a bath! Well, if my coat is smelly, that's probably a good thing.

I tell myself to concentrate so that I can read the minds of the people who are coming to look at the house. The woman is worrying about her hair. She is wondering if she needs more perfume. Her husband thinks he looks important, dressed in his suit. But our house is *not* a "suit-and-tie" house.

Simon and Kara are standing together
on the front lawn. Simon looks at his watch.

"They'll be here any minute," he says.

Any minute! It's time I made a move. I slip
into the house, ready for action.

First, I need to cover the house in dog hair.
I roll over and over and rub my back along the
carpet. I leave a trail of damp hairs behind me.
Great! Next, the sofa! Up I go! Rub! Rub!
This is fun! I'm never allowed up on the sofa!

Now, the window seat! This is absolutely not allowed. I leap up and rub myself all over the white cushions. Then I sit up and look out of the window. The glass is very clean! I press my wet nose all over the window, and rub my face from side to side. It leaves a nice big mark.

Quickly, I run into Marcus's room! I'm not a dog who breaks things, so I want to be very careful. I tug at the bedclothes and give the rug a quick kick. I pull the shoes out of the wardrobe and scatter them around. Then I pull out a pair of shorts from under the bed.

I hear a car door slam! I run out of the back door and around to the front garden. Simon and Kara are shaking hands with the buyers.

I have about ten seconds to complete my plan. I race to the garden by the front path and start digging up the flower bed. I dig and dig, leaving lots of mud all over the front step.

Then I run into my kennel. I put my head down and my paws over my ears – but I keep one eye open, just a little.

Chapter 4

DOGGY SMELLS

Oh dear! Now I'm chained to the kennel!

I haven't been tied up since I was a naughty pup. I have never known Simon and Kara to be so angry.

Surely they'll forgive me? Soon they'll be saying, "Thank goodness for Moby! If it hadn't been for him we might have sold our lovely home!" They'll laugh as they tell everyone about the bad smell in the house.

I close my eyes and think of yesterday, and how I got rid of those clean and fancy buyers.

I remember how Mrs Clean-and-Fancy walked up the dirty steps. Mr Clean-and-Fancy took her arm. I could tell that they were already having doubts about the house.

Inside, Mrs Clean-and-Fancy held a handkerchief to her nose. Never before have I been so proud of my doggy smells!

They were amazed by the mess in Marcus's bedroom. Mr and Mrs Clean-and-Fancy barely looked at the new wallpaper and curtains. They just stepped around the mess on the floor and turned to leave the room.

On her way out, Mrs Clean-and-Fancy caught the heel of her shoe in Marcus's shorts. There she was, hopping around the bedroom with the shorts looped over her foot. Oh, the joy of it!

Shortly afterwards, Kara offered them some tea.

"Please sit on the window seat," she urged. "It's such a lovely view from there. You can see the countryside."

Mrs Clean-and-Fancy didn't dare sit on the window seat. Not in her white skirt! Mr Clean-and-Fancy did look out through the window, but the view was very smudgy!

The buyers didn't stay for a cup of tea. They hurried out of the door, keen to be on their way.

Chapter 5

NEW PEOPLE - NEW PLAN

Simon and Kara are still not speaking to me. I'm not likely to get a bone tonight!

The house is all tidy again. Today, another couple is coming to look at it. I have a feeling they will be quiet, gentle folk. I've thought of a whole new plan to keep them from buying the house. This is a plan I can carry out even when I'm chained up in my kennel.

Impossible, you say? I don't think so!

First, I must contact my friend Buster.
Buster lives at the house over the back fence.
He's a fierce-looking dog but his bark is worse
than his bite. I sit quietly and I concentrate.
With my mind,
I tell Buster what
is happening at
our house and
what he can
do to help.

From over the fence, I hear Buster bark, just once. I can tell he has got my message.

Now for Lulu, who lives over the side fence. I'm sure she will help me. She won't want strangers moving in next to her! I send Lulu the same message and I hear her snuffling at the fence. Yes! She understands.

Over the road, there are two Dobermans – large black-and-brown dogs. They are well-behaved, and are no trouble to anyone. But I know that they are bored and looking for adventure. I'm sure they'll love to help with my plan.

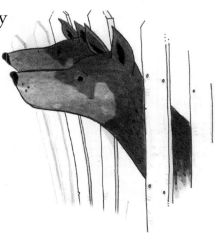

Then there's Albert, two doors down.
Albert is getting old.
He's very deaf but
he'll be able to read
my mind. I've heard
him bark too. What
a noise! I expect it's

because he can't hear himself, so he thinks
he needs to bark extra loudly!

We're almost ready to go. All I need is some
sort of signal to start it. A howl. That's it!
I love howling, but I don't often get the
chance to do it.

The people arrive to look at the house.
They *are* quiet people, people who like to stay
at home to make things, and to work in the
garden. They'll love our garden, I know it.

I quite like these new people, but I still
don't want to sell my house to them!

Inside, everything is tidy. Everything has
been vacuumed, washed and polished.

Kara and Simon are nervous. I can tell that they're wondering how long it will take to find a buyer for their house. But I'm too busy thinking about my plan to worry about what Simon and Kara are thinking.

Again, I must watch carefully, and wait for the right moment.

Chapter 6

A PROBLEM WITH DOGS

Simon and Kara are shaking the visitors' hands and everyone is smiling. Oh, no! These people are very kind and gentle. I can easily imagine them buying the house.

I watch Mr and Mrs Gentle wander down to the back of the garden.

"Perfect!" I hear Mr Gentle say as he looks at the shed. "I could make my pottery in here!"

Oh no! He really likes the house! This is getting serious. I want to do something – but not yet!

Inside the house, everything is perfect as well.

"The bedrooms are small, but we don't need much room," Mrs Gentle says. "I'll have one bedroom as an art studio."

I knew they would love the house!

I am getting anxious about my plan. I need Mr and Mrs Gentle to come outside again.

Yes! Here they are, at the door. They have one last look at the garden, and then they turn to shake hands with Simon and Kara.

"We'll be in touch," they say. "This house is just what we want. So peaceful!"

That's my cue. Peaceful, indeed! I raise my face and let out my loudest howl.

Suddenly, all the other dogs start barking too: Buster's woof, Lulu's yap, and the Dobermans' bark. Oh, what a wonderful sound!

Then Albert starts barking. He is amazing. His voice rises above the others – long, slow, deep barks!

Owwwwwww!

And me – well, I sit here as quiet as a mouse, not even wagging my tail. It's as though I haven't heard!

"Dogs!" cries Mrs Gentle. "Do you have a problem with dogs around here?"

Simon groans softly. He knows that these people are not going to buy the house now.

"Oh, no!" he answers desperately. "Dogs are never a problem. I can't imagine what's upset them today!"

I wag my tail and sit up straight with my head on one side as if to say, "Nothing to do with me!"

"We have cats!" Mrs Gentle says, quite loudly. "Three of them. I don't want to live in a neighbourhood where there are fierce dogs!"

"I'm sorry," adds Mr Gentle, quietly. "You can see that my wife is upset. She does worry about her cats. And, I think I'd find barking dogs difficult to live with too. Maybe we'd better find somewhere else to live."

Great! I think, as Mr and Mrs Gentle drive away.

As Kara turns around, I can see she is crying. "Oh, Simon," she whispers. "I really thought they would buy the house!"

Simon looks at me crossly. I know he is angry, but my plan has been a total success.

Chapter 7

A CHANGE OF HEART

This morning, Simon and Kara let me come back into the house, but only as far as the mat inside the door.

Simon is still angry. "It's Moby's fault no one will buy our house!" he mutters.

"Don't be silly, Simon," Kara says. "It's just our bad luck."

"That dog is doing it on purpose!" Simon
snaps back. "I don't know what's got into him!
Why should he care about where he lives?"

Oh dear! Now Kara is crying! I hate to see
her so upset.

"Simon," she sobs. "I really do want to live
by the beach, but I'm starting to think we'll
never be able to move!"

Oh, no! I didn't know they wanted to live by the beach. That sounds great! What have I done?

"Simon," Kara says. "Let's take Moby to see the house we want to live in."

"Well, it can't do any harm," says Simon. "Perhaps you're right."

"I think Moby's worried about moving," says Kara. "That might be why he's behaving so badly."

Behaving badly, indeed! But I wouldn't mind a trip to the seaside, so I quickly jump in the car.

As we travel, I know that Kara is thinking of the new house. It's a big house, with a huge garden rolling down towards the sea.

I think of how much fun Olivia and Marcus would have throwing sticks into the water. I'd love to swim out and fetch those sticks!

The car stops. Yes, that's the sea all right.
I can smell it, long before Simon opens the
car door to let me out.

"Here we are, Moby," Kara says. "If we
move, this will be our beach. See, that's the
house we want to buy, over there." She points
it out for me.

I can see the house through the trees.
I know it's the perfect place for us to live.
It will have a huge living room with a log fire
to sit by in the winter. Wonderful!

I run with Simon and Kara to the beach and dig in the sand. I race up and down by the water's edge. Kara and Simon laugh as they watch me play.

"We've got more people coming to see our house tomorrow, Moby," Kara shouts to me as I run up to her. "If we sell it, we can live here!"

Live here! Now I really want to do that! I wave my tail, showering them both with sand. I bark to tell them that we need to go home. I have a new plan to put in place.

Chapter 8

A NEW PLAN

I've come up with a great new plan. I'm doing everything right today. I'm showing a lovely young couple through the house.

"What a sweet dog," the woman says. "We're going to get a dog. I hope it will be as friendly as Moby," she laughs, as she pats me.

We have to wait until tomorrow to find out if they are going to buy the house. Kara and Simon are nervous, but I know that Mr and Mrs Young Couple are going to buy it.

Tonight I'm allowed inside to lie on the carpet. Luxury! I close my eyes and dream of living by the beach. I dream of waves splashing onto the shore. In my dreams, I hear someone calling a dog.

"Stella! Come on, girl!" calls a boy about Marcus's age. "Come and meet Moby! He's your new neighbour."

I wake up, but in my mind I can still see Stella. She's beautiful!

"Stella," I sigh. Perfect! Stella and Moby! The names go so well together.

I'm happy not to be called Jack after all!